Duncan and Trevor Smith are son and fatl  co-written book. Their previous works include *Yorkshire Curiosities* (1992) and *North and East York* by The Dovecote Press. In 1997 they self-publi Press) to which *More Sheffield Curiosities* is the seq approaching the 30,000 mark. Together they have contributed numerous articles to the *Dalesman* magazine and have lectured widely across the county.

Duncan Smith was born in Sheffield in 1960. From the age of ten he has been an avid collector of all things historical, going on to read Ancient History and Archaeology at Birmingham University. A keen traveller, gardener and book collector, he currently works in the publishing industry. In 1995 he wrote *Yorkshire: A Portrait in Colour* (The Dovecote Press) which received widespread critical acclaim.

Trevor Smith of Scottish extraction, was born in Sheffield in 1921. He has had a varied career, including some eight years of teaching and many more in public and university libraries. He has a lifelong interest in freelance writing and photography and for some considerable time has been compiling a list of curiosities of the British Isles. His other interests include military history and English and American literature.

Press Reviews:
"An entertaining look at 82 of the county's odder corners" SOUTH AND WEST YORKSHIRE CURIOSITIES *(Sheffield Star)*

"all things weird and wonderful. . . full of daft bits and pieces" NORTH AND EAST YORKSHIRE CURIOSITIES *(Sheffield Star)*

"excellent photographs. . . elegant and informative text. . . everyone will find a few surprises here." YORKSHIRE: A PORTRAIT IN COLOUR *(Yorkshire Journal)*

"more than 200 photographs of the best of Yorkshire" YORKSHIRE: A PORTRAIT IN COLOUR *(Yorkshire Life)*

"a book for the explorer, whether on foot, by transport or in an armchair" SHEFFIELD CURIOSITIES *(Sheffield History Reporter)*

Overleaf: Sculpture in Sheffield Cathedral to the crews of HMS Sheffield, unveiled in 2000 by HRH The Duke of York (see No.48)

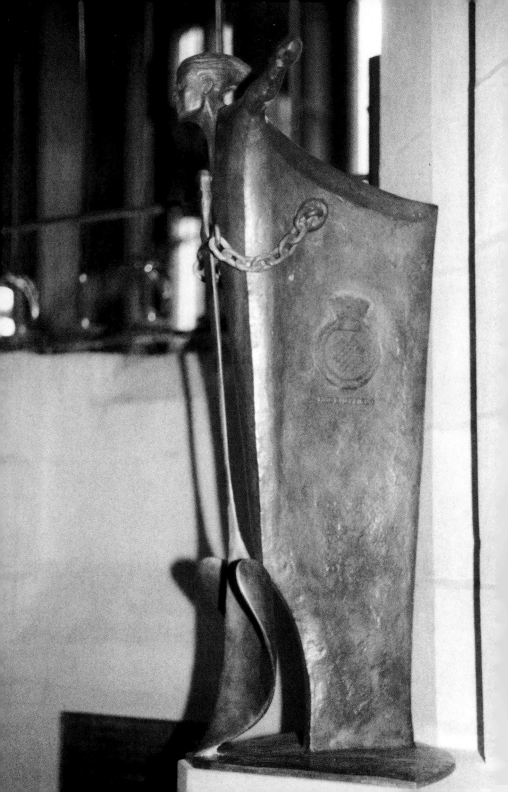

MORE SHEFFIELD CURIOSITIES

Duncan & Trevor Smith

H·E·D·G·E·R·O·W

publishing ltd

Monument to sculptor Godfrey Sykes, Weston Park (see no.41)

"For Mary, Catherine, Adrian and Roswitha"

Photo credits: Duncan Smith (all photos);
except ©2000 Hedgerow Publishing Ltd. (front cover), Jane Hale (no.32), Roswitha Reisinger
(no.47, back cover top and second down), Trevor Smith (nos.25, 27, 28 and 55)
& The Sheffield Postcard Co. (nos.15, 29, and 46)
Illustrations of the Lavender Fairy and the Pear Blossom Fairy (no.33) by Cicely
Mary Barker. Copyright © The Estate of Cicely Mary Barker 1940, 1944.
Reproduced with kind permission of Frederick Warne & Co.

First Published in 2000 by
Hedgerow Publishing Ltd., 325 Abbeydale Road, Sheffield S7 1FS,
South Yorkshire, England

ISBN 1–872740–01–4

Typeset by Hedgerow Publishing Ltd.
Printed and bound in Worksop, Nottinghamshire

INTRODUCTION

When "Sheffield Curiosities" was first published in 1997 it was an immediate success with both the public and the press. So much so that it prompted a second impression in 1999 with a new preface which updated the first edition, as well as listing a few new additions. During this time we received numerous kind letters from readers suggesting further local oddities. We also lectured regularly around the City during which audience members were eager to ask if we had seen this or that. With a growing list of new curiosities to hand we were soon mooting the idea of writing "More Sheffield Curiosities" - and work began in earnest. No sooner had we started than curiosities, previously missed or omitted due to space, started cropping up all over the place. As always, the local press proved a valuable hunting ground, both in terms of reports and readers' letters. Of the many invaluable local history books consulted, the reader wishing to dig deeper will find a bibliography at the back of this book. We are also indebted to Mr. Peter Carter of High Storrs. His numerous letters and photographs over the last year or so have brought several curiosities to our attention which would otherwise have gone unnoticed.

As with its predecessor, the aim of "More Sheffield Curiosities" is "to trawl this rich and chequered heritage for tangible remains of Sheffield's bygone days". These survivals, or 'curiosities', can be as modest as village stocks and wall plaques, or as obvious as monuments and listed buildings. What connects them all is that each has a story to tell and a part to play in the historical development of a great city.

Duncan and Trevor Smith, Sheffield, 2000

CONTENTS

MAP SHOWING THE LOCATION OF MORE
SHEFFIELD CURIOSITIES

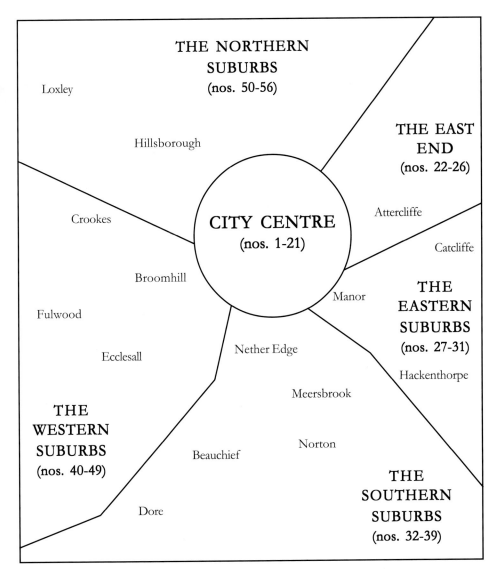

THE NORTHERN
SUBURBS
(nos. 50-56)

Loxley

Hillsborough

THE EAST
END
(nos. 22-26)

Crookes

CITY CENTRE
(nos. 1-21)

Attercliffe

Catcliffe

Broomhill

Manor

THE
EASTERN
SUBURBS
(nos. 27-31)

Fulwood

Ecclesall

Nether Edge

Hackenthorpe

Meersbrook

THE
WESTERN
SUBURBS
(nos. 40-49)

Beauchief

Norton

THE
SOUTHERN
SUBURBS
(nos. 32-39)

Dore

(The authors recommend that a detailed Sheffield street map plan is used to pinpoint curiosities when visiting. For maps showing bygone Sheffield, the Alan Godfrey series of reproduction old maps is fascinating.)

1. Under the Watchful Gaze of Chaucer

EAST PARADE, S1

The flamboyant Tudor-style red-brick building on the corner of High Street and East Parade was designed by the architect M.E.Hadfield in 1883 (see back cover second down). It was the first of the impressive late Victorian facades which eventually dominated this part of the city centre. Called Parade Chambers, it was constructed for Pawson and Brailsford whose thriving business was founded on stationery, commercial printing and colour lithography. A flick through the pages of their *"Illustrated Guide to Sheffield"* (1862) demonstrates why they had a national reputation. Their new premises were several storeys high, the upper floors being rented out to solicitors and accountants. The facade is superbly decorated with renaissance and ecclesiastical details, such as medieval-style gargoyles. This acknowledged the parish church, whose gates once stood outside the door, and the status of Henry Pawson as Churchwarden. Notable amongst the sculptures are busts of Chaucer, author of *"The Canterbury Tales"*, and Caxton, inventor of the printing press. Carved initials identify them, as the carved "P&B" identifies whose building it was.

2. Disraeli's Lord Chancellor
CHURCH STREET, S1

Towards the upper end of Church Street is a finely constructed, red brick Victorian building with an interesting history. Built in 1894-96 as the offices for Henry and Alfred Maxfield, solicitors, this ornate building bears the name Cairns Chambers. It was named after Hugh McCalmont Cairns, Lord Chancellor in Prime Minister Disraeli's government (1868 and 1874-80), and one of the greatest lawyers of the nineteenth century. His statue can still be seen in a canopied niche over the entrance. It is said that in order to ensure the Lord Chancellor's robes were modelled correctly, the sculptor, Frank Tory, hired a set from London for a guinea a day! Tory was a local craftsman responsible for the carving on this and several other buildings in the city designed by Charles Hadfield. Cairns Chambers is in the mock-Tudor Gothic style which was one of Hadfield's favourites. On the corner of the building is a sundial inscribed "Tempus Fugit" (Time Flies). Closeby are the carved heads of the Prince and Princess of Wales (later Edward VII and Queen Alexandra).

3. Meet Me at Cole's Corner

FARGATE, S1

Some older Sheffielders still refer to the corner of Church Street and Fargate as 'Cole's Corner', even though the magnificent store erected by one of the town's leading drapers was demolished nearly 40 years ago. Cole Brothers was originally founded by three brothers in premises at the bottom of Fargate in 1847. By 1869 their success enabled them to build their new corner-site store on a palatial scale which set it quite apart. However, by the turn of the century much of Fargate and High Street had been re-developed, and all the principal stores were now 5 or 6 storeys high. Cole's Corner soon became a popular meeting place where many young couples reputedly met on their first date. Eventually, even Cole's Corner grew old-fashioned and the shop re-located in 1963 to new premises in Barker's Pool. The site had originally been occupied by the Albert Hall cinema which had burnt down in 1937. The only momento of Cole's Corner to-day is a plaque on the modern building which now occupies the site.

4. A Clutch of Cathedral Curiosities
CHURCH STREET, S1

Churches and cathedrals provide particularly happy hunting grounds for the curiosity seeker. Primarily they are more than often ancient buildings, often on the site of earlier structures, whose fabric and accumulated treasures have been venerated across the centuries. Sheffield's Cathedral Church of St Peter and St Paul is no exception. Worship on this site has been traced back as far as Saxon times (see No.40) although the present Gothic church was begun in c.1430. It has been added to ever since and was raised to Cathedral status in 1913. Visitors may wish to seek out the bust of the Rev. James Williamson, the first work in marble by Sheffield sculptor Francis Chantrey. There is a wooden preaching desk reputed to have been used by John Wesley, as depicted on a stained glass window in the Chapter House (both may be viewed by appointment only). A blocked doorway at the junction of the choir and transept is said to have been used 'anonymously' by Mary Queen of Scots. An interesting tablet to one William Watson (d.1793) shows him to have been the first of 23 children and the longest living! Hanging in St George's Chapel is the ensign of the first HMS Sheffield while her bell is at the west end of the nave (see No.48). Finally, the Lady Chapel is worth a detour to marvel at its unusual carved roof bosses depicting the Mother Goddess and the 'Green Man'.

5. An Early Private Bank
HARTSHEAD, S1

Standing in what was once Hartshead Square is a grand three-story brick house built in 1728 by merchant Nicholas Broadbent. A lead drain pipe still bears his initials at roof level. His son Joseph built a row of houses in the 1730's which later became the north side of Paradise Square. However, it was left to his grandson Thomas to really make a name for the family by founding one of the earliest private banks. This he did in 1771 in the house on Hartshead, which has since always been known as the Old Bank House. After a promising start he began work in earnest on a new house called Page Hall. Unfortunately the bank failed in the 1780's with considerable debts. The Hall passed eventually to steel magnate Mark Firth who created Firth Park from its extensive grounds. Although the Old Bank House no longer stands in its own gardens and is now offices, it is still an imposing building which played a significant part in the early development of Sheffield town. Of a similar date is the former Sheffield Banking Co. Ltd. building on George Street.

6. Sheffield's First Hospital For Women
FIG TREE LANE, S1

A stroll up and down the numerous steep little roads that run from Campo Lane/ Hartshead down to West Bar reveals an undisturbed corner of old Sheffield town. Many of the buildings have tales to tell, while others, such as that carved with Hebrew text from the Bible on North Church Street, only beg questions from the curiosity hunter. There is no confusion, however, over the original use of Victoria Chambers on Fig Tree Lane. This splendid building with its columned porch and pilastered south front has a plaque identifying it as Sheffield's first hospital solely for women. It was opened with 12 beds in the early 1860's by Doctors Aveling, Jackson and Keeling. Now housing a law firm, it retains numerous original internal features including a fine circular staircase. In 1878 it was replaced by the new Jessop Hospital For Women founded by steel magnate Thomas Jessop on Leavygreave Road.

7. A Rooftop Playground
EAST PARADE, S1

Years ago, when Sheffield was a town, the city centre included not just shops and offices, but private houses, workshops and even schools. The casual shopper today would be unaware that much remained from these times unless they looked upwards. For example on Cambridge Street can be found an old brick building identified only by a datestone high up in the wall inscribed "Bethel Sunday School 1872". Even more fascinating is a building at the north end of East Parade, adorned with the Royal coat of arms and with railings around its roof on the York Street side. This was once the Boys' Charity School, built in 1825, and the railings enclosed their rooftop playground. The boys used to play in the nearby parish churchyard (now the Cathedral) but, after objections from the churchwardens, they were confined to their roof! In 1911 they moved to a new school on Psalter Lane, now the School of Art, where they could roam free at ground level! Also of educational interest is the old Charity School for Poor Girls on St James' Row. The former medical school on Leopold Street has a door above which is carved "ARS LONGA VITA BREVIS". Opposite is the former Firth College opened in 1879 by Prince Leopold. Over the doorway are sculptures representing Science and Art.

8. The Home of Sheffield's Newspapers
HARTSHEAD, S1

High on the wall of the modern Sheffield Newspapers building, on the corner of Hartshead and Aldine Court, is a stone plaque. It tells us that here stood the office of the *Sheffield Iris*, Sheffield's first true newspaper. In 1787 the building had become Joseph Gales' stationery shop where he printed his radical *Sheffield Register*. Gales fled to America in 1794 because of his unpopular views on the French Revolution; James Montgomery, a Scot, took over and renamed the newspaper the *Iris*. He composed hymns and poems in a back room bringing him an international audience. He was also a philanthropic man being involved in many charitable activities. After his death in 1854 he was remembered by a fine statue, now within the Cathedral grounds, a drinking fountain in Broad Lane, and had a hall, a road and several pubs named after him. His premises became one of these pubs but this was later demolished, parts being sold to Americans as souvenirs of Gales. On Watson's Walk, leading to nearby Angel Street, is another plaque, to William Marsden (1796-1867), who was born closeby. He studied at St Bartholomews Hospital and became a member of the Royal College of Surgeons in 1827. In 1828 he founded the country's first free hospital and in 1851 opened what became the Royal Marsden cancer hospital.

9. An Early Form of House Insurance

WEST BAR, S3

Sheffield can be justifiably proud of its state-of-the-art fire station and fire service headquarters on Carver Street. It is a far cry indeed from the mid-14th century when the only fire fighting equipment available consisted of leather buckets hanging at a few key locations! The first fire engine was not purchased until 1703. The fascinating history of Sheffield's fire service is illustrated at the excellent South Yorkshire Fire Service Museum. The museum occupies the former West Bar Fire Station, opened in 1900, where the first motorised engine was housed in 1907. Some of the smallest but most interesting exhibits are the metal plaques known as "Fire marks", removed from various buildings in the city. Before the Town Council took over the Fire Service in 1869, property-owners had to pay a premium to insure against fire. In return they received a "fire mark" which they attached to their building. In the event of a fire, the relevant Insurance Brigade would turn out, check for the fire mark and deal with the blaze. Uninsured properties were only attended on payment of a charge. Also of interest is the highest continuous "pole-drop" in the country and the plaster facade of John Watts Cutlers next to the carpark.

(N.B: The Museum is open Sundays 11am-5pm and is run entirely by volunteers.)

10. A Monument in Bricks and Mortar
SNIG HILL, S3

Two things can be said of the City of Sheffield. Firstly, it is a world-ranking producer of steel, and secondly, it has a dearth of monumental sculpture in its centre. It is perhaps fitting then, that one of the city's first modern public artworks is a four-storey brick mural of a steelworker (*see front cover*). It was commissioned by the City Council in 1986 to cover a gable-end and is based on an image by artist Paul Waplington. The mural, which uses 30,000 bricks of 18 different types, pays homage to the achievements of Sheffield's great steel heritage. Of similar construction is a gable-end mural at Hallam University, this time depicting a group of vultures! Perhaps more relevant is the fine sculpture of crucible steel workers to be found inside the Meadowhall shopping centre. They are curious, however, because crucible steel was never produced on this site. Also eye-catching is the giant metal spider by sculptor Johnny White on a wall on Savile Street East. Returning to the city centre, except for Edward VII in Fitzalan Square, all the old monumental sculptures have been removed to the suburbs. However, the following modern works are worth looking for: George Fullard's modern figures in front of the Upper Chapel, Norfolk Street; some novel inscribed metal balconies on Rockingham Street; Mick Farrell's "Sheen" on Howard Street (in memory of Marti Caine) and David Kemp's hulking "Heavy Plant" in the Science Park nearby; Brian Asquith's "Elements Fire Steel" on the wall of Hallam University's Howard Building; the cutlery freize on the White Building (1908) in Fitzalan Square; David Wynne's "Horse and Rider" off Barker's Pool; and Paula Haughney's "The Gift" outside The Crucible.

11. The Origin of Wednesday and United

TUDOR SQUARE, S1

On the site now occupied by the Crucible Theatre there once stood The Adelphi Hotel. It was here in 1854, according to a Rotary Heritage plaque, that the Duke of Norfolk's agent announced that the Duke supported the idea of a cricket ground at Bramall Lane. The first match was played in April 1855 and so the Sheffield United Cricket Club was born. In March 1889 it was suggested that a football club should run alongside the cricket club, and so Sheffield United Football Club came into being. On 5th September 1867 another meeting took place at the Adelphi. This time Sheffield Wednesday Football Club was formed, in order to keep the old Wednesday Cricket Club together over the winter. Formed originally in 1820, the cricket club was named 'Wednesday' as this was the day taken off by the 'little mesters' to watch the cricket! The world's first football club was the Sheffield Football Club founded in 1857, at a meeting held in a greenhouse! The second oldest is the Hallam Football Club, founded in 1860, making its Sandygate ground the world's oldest.

Opposite the Crucible is a plaque to Sheffield film pioneer Frank Mottershaw (1850-1932) whose studio once stood here.

12. A Sculpted Shrine to Government
PINSTONE STREET, S1

It is often said that the centre of Sheffield lacks any significant large-scale sculpture, other than the statue of Edward VII in Fitzalan Square. This dearth, however, is compensated for by a growing body of modern civic artworks (see no. 10) and an oft-overlooked array of small Victorian architectural sculptures (eg. the curious miniatures depicting the creation around the former YMCA on the corner of Fargate and Norfolk Row; also the symbols on "The Surrey" public house, once a freemasons' meeting place). However, Sheffield's sculpted jewel must surely be the Grade 1 listed Town Hall on Pinstone Street. How easy it is to take this Gothic masterpiece for granted and to miss its myriad carvings and statues. Opened by Queen Victoria on 21st May 1897 and designed by E.W. Mountford in "a free northern Renaissance style" it is a mass of gables, mullioned windows and copper-roofed turrets. On one corner is an imposing tower 180 feet high and topped with an 8 foot high bronze statue of Vulcan standing on an anvil, a symbol of Sheffield's prowess in metal manufacture. On the Pinstone Street facade is a statue of Queen Victoria and in the foyer another of the Duke of Norfolk, first Lord Mayor of Sheffield. The front elevation has a frieze depicting Sheffield's many crafts and industries together with the city's arms. More curious are the carved owl and pelican, not to mention the word "Disinfectants" over a door on Norfolk Street!

The old Town Hall on Waingate is a more sombre affair enlivened by a splendid public water fountain on Castle Street.

13. The New Peace Gardens
PINSTONE STREET, S1

Judging by the number of people walking around Sheffield's redeveloped Peace Gardens, in both sun and rain, this latest chapter in Sheffield's city centre redevelopment is a popular one. However, amidst the waterfalls, walkways and fountains are a number of monuments which, whilst not necessarily curious, are certainly interesting. It was heartening to see that the fascinating Imperial Standard Measures have been moved from their old home on St Paul's Parade to a site adjacent to the Town Hall. The old plaque to Samuel Holberry (1814-42), Sheffield's Chartist leader, has been replaced by a crisp new stone inscription. Of equal quality is an engraved memorial to Sheffielders who served in the Spanish Civil War (1936-39). It includes these stirring lines from Byron: "Yet, freedom yet, thy banner torn but flying, streams like a thunderstorm against the wind." On a similar theme is the Hiroshima Memorial Stone which was originally unveiled on Hiroshima Day, 8th August 1985, in the presence of three survivors of the atomic devastation. Finally, at the time of writing, it has been agreed to erect a further plaque, this time to those Sheffield citizens who gave their lives in all conflicts, including the Korean War.

14. By Royal Appointment
LEOPOLD STREET, S1

The area around the Town Hall, itself opened officially by Queen Victoria (see no. 12), has numerous royal connections. Leopold Street was so named after Prince Leopold, who visited Sheffield in 1879 to open Firth College in a fine building which still stands at the corner with West Street. This led eventually to the creation of Sheffield University on Western Bank. On the corner with Barker's Pool is a grand building which today is home to a jeweller. It was built originally in 1884 for Johnson and Appleyard, cabinet makers who enjoyed Royal Appointment. To this day, high up on the facade, is a stone which reads "Cabinet makers by appointment to the Prince of Wales". Later the building was named Beethoven House, being home to the piano firm of John Peck and Arthur Wilson, created in the early 1890's. Next door once existed The Cinema House where those two "royals" from the entertainment world, Laurel and Hardy, appeared on a flying visit in 1932.

15. A Tall Order!
BARKER'S POOL, S1

The centre of Barker's Pool is dominated by a flagpole which must surely be one of the tallest, single-piece steel monuments in the world. Together with a striking sculptured bronze base and granite plinth it makes up the city's official war memorial. A competition to design the memorial had been held in 1924 and was won by Charles D. Carus-Wilson, head of the University's Department of Architecture. Although Carus-Wilson suggested wood, the 90 feet high 'Venetian' mast was eventually rendered in steel. It was unveiled on October 28th 1925 by Lt.-Gen. Sir Charles Harrington. Surprisingly the pole, which weighed 10 tons, was manufactured in Hull. Its huge length posed many problems on its way up from the old Wicker Goods Station, and was undertaken after midnight when traffic was at a minimum.

Barker's Pool, Sheffield. 6249.

16. From Water to Watering Hole
DIVISION STREET, S1

The grand old building on the corner of Division and Holly Street has had a long and curious history. It was built in 1867 to a design by Flockton and Abbot for the Sheffield Water Company. The name, flanked by carvings of water gods, can still be seen. The Town Council acquired the company in 1887. In c.1900 the building became headquarters for J.G. Graves' mail-order business, the largest in the British Empire. At its peak it employed 3,000 Sheffielders, moving to new offices on Durham Road in 1903. Graves started out as a watchmaker's apprentice and eventually became Lord Mayor of Sheffield. He was also a great philanthropist responsible for Graves Park and Graves Art Gallery. The building was later used by Sheffield Transport Department, the N.U.M. and has today, like so many other old buildings, become a fashionable bar. Interestingly, the water offices are echoed down on Commercial Street by the former offices of the Sheffield United Gaslight Company (see pg. 64). Built in 1874 to a design by M.E. Hadfield and Son, it has pink granite columns outside and a superb glass dome in the General Office. The ceiling still carries the words "smokeless fuel" in Latin! The company later became the Sheffield and District Gas Co., the largest provincial gas company in Britain.

17. The Stamp of Approval
PORTOBELLO STREET, S1

For 700 years, Sheffield and cutlery have been synonymous and what better way to celebrate this than by taking a look at the Cutlers' Hall on Church Street. Though not a curiosity in itself this splendid edifice, home to the 'Company of Cutlers in Hallamshire', does contain the famous 80-blade 'Norfolk Knife'. It was made by Joseph Rodgers and Sons for the Great Exhibition in 1851 and was 2 years in the making! Far less grand, but more curious, is the Assay Office on Portobello Street. In 1773 the Birmingham Assay Office was created by Act of Parliament. With the introduction of Old Sheffield Plate and a resulting increase in silver work an assay office was opened in Sheffield. Its function was to test that articles of silver (and later gold and platinum) came up to prescribed standards as stipulated by "The Guardians of the standard of wrought plate within the town of Sheffield". Originally located in Leopold Street (1880-1958), it then moved to a modern building on Portobello Street. Above the doorway is a carved crown and a York Rose, the symbols which were used to hallmark Sheffield silver and gold respectively. The carved letter 'Q' denotes the year of construction (1958), in the same way as it denoted the year of manufacture on silver. An extension to the building in 1978 is likewise adorned with a carved letter 'D'.

18. Sheffield's Biggest Advertisement
DEVONSHIRE STREET, S1

Sheffield's steel industry required large quantities of refractory clay to make Huntsman's crucibles and to line Bessemer converters, amongst other things. This 'fireclay', as it is known, occurs near the western edge of the coal measures, in the Deepcar area. Prominent in the fireclay industry was John Armitage who bought an existing works in the 1850's and then expanded rapidly at Station Road, Deepcar. Like other former fireclay works in the area little or nothing remains of those mines other than the occasional spoilheap and associated workers' cottages. However, John Armitage and Sons specialised in decorative moulded fireclay bricks and ornamental figures, designed by artist Peter Nanetti. In order to market these succesfully they built a showroom on Devonshire Street in 1888 which survives today. The exuberant decoration of the exterior walls incorporates many examples of the company's work, thus acting as a colossal advertisement in itself, to be marvelled at by passers-by. It is tempting to think that the curious heads we described in our previous book ("Sheffield Curiosities" p.34) originated here.

19. A Kangaroo, a Dog and a Tiger
WELLINGTON STREET, S1

Despite the wholesale re-development of great tracts of Sheffield's city centre, the curiosity-hunter can still find fascinating untouched pockets of Victorian industry. Admittedly these former works are either empty or re-used, but their exuberant facades bear witness to a prosperous past. For a good impression of the layout of these one-time hives of industry take a look at the Alpha Works on Carver Street, Leah's Yard on Cambridge Street and, best of all, Butcher Works off Arundel Street. Such was the success of Mr. Butcher that he went to Philadelphia and produced the first steel castings to be manufactured commercially in the USA! Occasionally, the usual combination of brick-built facade with grand entrance is enlivened by the inclusion of the company's trademark. On Wellington Street, for instance, can be seen a superb carved kangaroo logo. Similarly, on West Street, the Tiger Works is adorned with that beast and on Bailey Lane is a pointer dog over the door. The Meersbrook Works on Valley Road bears the "three legs of Man", the Insignia Works on Rutland Road has a "hand and heart" and the Globe Works on Alma Street has a carved globe. Also of interest is the name "Meersbrook Tannery" at 41-65 Chesterfield Road where leather drive belts were made; the tiled galloping horse at Stokes Paints on Little London Road; the "Royal Appointment" crest on Brindley and Foster's organ works on Suffolk Road; and the modest inscription of "H.W. Roberts, Memorial Works" at the top of Granville Road.

20. A Revolutionary Factory Building
MOORE STREET, S3

As a major industrial city it is not surprising that some of Sheffield's factory buildings incorporated structural features which were revolutionary at the time. A good example of this was on the corner of Moore Street and Young Street. The flamboyant entrance with its elaborate terracotta ornament led into one of the most advanced industrial buildings in the city. It was built in 1908 for Joseph Pickering and Sons as a box-making factory. The designers, C & C.M.E. Hadfield, used the then new combination of a steel framework with concrete floors. This minimized any risk of fire spreading through the building. It could not, however, prevent the bulldozers reducing it to rubble recently in order that the decorative facade be re-used as a front for a suite of new offices. More conventional is the Eyewitness Works on nearby Milton Street. It is curious however, for a cornerstone inscribed painstakingly with a prayer, probably by an employee over many lunch breaks!

21. The Scottish Brewer in Sheffield
BROWN STREET, S1

Brewing has had a long and fascinating history in Sheffield although few tangible remains exist today. One such survival is the name "DUNCAN GILMOUR & CO. LIMITED" along the facade of The Rutland Arms on Brown Street. Not surprisingly the company was founded by a Scot, in 1831, as a wines and spirits merchant. They began brewing in 1860 on Furnival Gate and purchased W.H. Birk's Lady's Bridge Brewery on Bridge Street in 1900. Gilmour's soon became Sheffield's second largest brewery, after Tennant Brothers. They took over several other breweries including High House Brewery on Bamforth Street, off Penistone Road, for use as a bottling plant. These buildings are still visible today. Eventually in 1954 the company, together with its 350 pubs, was itself taken over by Leeds brewers Joshua Tetley & Sons Ltd., becoming a distribution depot. When a new depot opened off Herries Road the old brewery was demolished becoming the site of the new Magistrates Court. The name of Duncan Gilmour had passed into the history books.

22. Sheffield's 'Titanic' Connection

SAVILE STREET, S4

The facade, main entrance and distinctive tower of Ward's Albion Works is one of the unmistakeable landmarks of Sheffield's old East End. Thomas W. Ward had set up as a local merchant in 1878 and quickly expanded into industrial demolition and the scrap trade, as well as railway engineering. In the 1890's the company began shipbreaking at Barrow-in-Furness and elsewhere. By the twentieth century the company was active across a whole range of industries including iron, steel, engineering, quarrying, plant hire and cement. Part of the facade still includes the words "KETTON CEMENT STORE". Most impressive is the pedimented office block with a portico of polished granite from their De Lank quarry in Cornwall. Many of the original fittings including ornate banisters, fine panelling, stained glass and chandeliers came from the ships they broke up. Notably, the boardroom's wood panelling once belonged to the first class cabins of the S.S. Olympic. She was sister ship to the ill-fated White Star liner Titanic which sank in 1912 with such tragic loss of life (some second class cabin panelling ended up in the Cutlers' Hall). Although closed in 1983, successor firms now occupy the old works including the local Chamber of Commerce.

23. The Victorian Vestry
BURNGREAVE ROAD, S3

A 'vestry' was originally a small room attached to a church in which vestments were stored. However, throughout the Victorian period in Sheffield the vestry became an important centre of local power. Civil vestries, as they were known, played a considerable part in government of the suburbs, alongside the town council. A Board of Guardians met regularly to discuss parish business such as the maintenance of local roads and the collection of rates for the poor. Such was their power that magnificent vestry offices were specially built, some of which remain today, albeit now used for other purposes. Notable is the listed Vestry Office for Brightside township at Burngreave, erected in 1864. Others can be seen on Cemetery Road (Ecclesall), Crookesmoor Road (Nether Hallam) and Attercliffe Common (Attercliffe-cum-Darnall).

24. Attercliffe's Corn Mill
BIRCH ROAD, S9

It is hard to imagine that Attercliffe was ever anything other than the built-up area we see today. However, back in 1805, in what was then a rural setting, a steam-powered corn mill was built. The mill itself has long gone, and the area been built up, but the Manager's house can still be seen, set back slightly on Birch Road. With its fine ashlar masonry and bay windows, the building seems incongruous amidst the factories and works buildings. The house later became a free dispensary, a foundry workers' club, a Caribbean community centre and is today a snooker club. Also of interest, a little further down the road, is an old brick-built factory dated 1911. Incorporated into the facade are the initials "I & C" and a pair of spectacles!

25. The Quaker Clockmaker
COLERIDGE ROAD, S9

By 1716 blister steel was being produced in Sheffield by a German process known as the "cementation process". When bars of it were forged under a tilt hammer it became shear steel, which was better than iron but still uneven in composition. It needed heating up to 1600°C to remedy this which was made possible by the use of clay crucibles. This was the brainchild of Benjamin Huntsman (1704-76), a Quaker clockmaker from Doncaster. Crucible steel proved ideal for tools and special steels because the process enabled composition and quality to be controlled. So successful was it that by the 1840's Sheffield made half of the world's crucible steel and new furnaces were built right up to the Great War, when new techniques were developed. Of Huntsman's first two works in Attercliffe sadly nothing remains. However, on Coleridge Road can be seen the remains of the Huntsman Works built in 1899, with a fine broad chimney above a 24-hole crucible shop. The East End is still littered with equally important industrial remains although few are signposted or cared for. One that has received a plaque is the former Firth Brown Research Laboratories on Princess Street where chromium-nickel steel, widely used today, was developed.

26. An Ancient British Fortress
JENKIN ROAD, S9

Today's visitors to Sheffield's Don Valley will find a bustling area dominated by the great retail edifice that is the Meadowhall Shopping Centre. However, in ancient times the valley was empty, and looming over it was the Wincobank Hill Fort. It's still there today although far less dominant due to the incursion of roads and modern housing. The explorer should not be disheartened and is advised to make his or her ascent via Tipton Street and Jenkin Road. The fort consisted of two circular ditches with wooden palisading, the lower one now concealed by houses. The upper one, however, can still be traced around the top of the hill, from where superb views of the surrounding area may be gained. No wonder the ancient British tribe the Brigantes chose this particular site for their fortress. Unfortunately few finds have ever been discovered to give an accurate date for construction. Running north-eastwards is an associated trackway known confusingly as the 'Roman Ridge' but in reality also pre-Roman in date. In the last war the fort was home to an anti-aircraft gun and searchlight emplacement, the base of which still remains.

27. England's Largest Listed Building
SOUTH STREET, S2

First proposed in the late 1950's and completed in 1961, Park Hill flats brought international fame to Sheffield, being the most dramatic example of mass public housing in post-war Britain. It occupies a dramatic location on a hillside east of the city centre and is notable for its bold use of exposed concrete. The complex was designed by city architect J.L. Womersley and based on pioneering work by Swiss architect Le Corbusier. The idea was to re-create the community spirit of the old dilapidated terraced streets which it replaced, by the use of wide walkways, or decks. Using the sloping topography of the site the decks gave access to the majority of flats from ground level. They also encouraged social interaction of the occupants unlike the disastrous craze for tower blocks. These "streets in the air" included shops, schools, pubs and a community centre for the three and a half thousand occupants of the 995 flats. All their refuse was flushed away to a central incinerator which helped keep them warm. Today the Park Hill flats have a Grade II* listing making it England's largest listed building. The fabric is being repaired by the City Council and English Heritage. The taller and less succesful Hyde Park flats adjacent have largely been demolished.

28. The Earl of Shrewsbury's Hospital
NORFOLK ROAD, S2

In the Middle Ages wealthy church and lay men sometimes provided specially built accommodation for the local aged and infirm. These establishments, which usually consisted of a group of houses and a chapel, are known as almshouses or hospitals. The Earl of Shrewsbury's hospital was originally built in 1665 near Park Square, for men and women "reduced by misfortune". However, due to repeated flooding by the River Sheaf, the building was demolished in 1827 and a new one erected opposite the Cholera Garden on Norfolk Road. The fine range of buildings could accommodate twenty men and twenty women, each receiving a weekly allowance plus coal and clothing periodically. Even to-day, although surrounded by the modern city, the Shrewsbury Hospital retains an air of almost monastic calm. It has been estimated that there are some 2,500 almshouses in England yet no two were ever built quite the same (see nos. 38 and 45).

29. The Queen's Tower
PARK GRANGE ROAD, S2

Squeezed into a less than glamorous space between Park Grange Road and East Bank Road is one of Sheffield's most romantic buildings. Queen's Tower is a mock castle designed in a 'Tudor-Gothic' style by the architect M. E. Hadfield. It was erected in the 1830's for the prosperous silverware manufacturer and philanthropist Samuel Roberts. The castellated towers, turrets and gateways reflect Roberts' romantic fascination for Mary, Queen of Scots who had been held captive at Sheffield Manor. Such was his disgust that the Manor now lay in ruins, he acquired a wall and window from it which he rebuilt in his grounds. Thus, it is all the more tragic that the Queen's Tower itself now lies empty and awaiting re-use. Its once splendid gardens, laid out by Robert Marnock, have now been obscured by the Norfolk Park estate, and yet despite all this, the building still retains a magical air about it. Roberts never actually lived here, instead presenting it to his only son, Samuel, when he married. Roberts Snr. died in 1848 aged 86 and is buried at Aston.
(NB. There is no public access at present to Queen's Tower and its grounds).

30. A Heritage Park

GRANVILLE ROAD, S2

Within living memory Norfolk Park was still one of Sheffield's most popular green spaces. Some can still recall the annual Whitsuntide hymn singing, community bonfires and the national Milk Race for cyclists. It is fitting therefore that, after years of neglact, the area has now been designated a "Heritage Park" which will be re-generated to engage the community once more. Also of interest, however, are the numerous associated park structures including Grade II listed lodges, a fine lamp standard at the Granville Road entrance and the preserved former entrance to the café. Most noteworthy is the west lodge at the lower entrance, on Norfolk Park Road. It has a rustic porch which was once inscribed "God bless the Queen and the Howards - 1857". The Queen was Victoria and the Howards were the Dukes of Norfolk, one of whom presented the park to the City in 1909.

31. Monuments to an Important Sheffield Family

HANDSWORTH ROAD, S13

On the roadside, at the corner of Handsworth Road and Richmond Road, can be found an old nineteenth century combined horse trough and drinking fountain. It is all the more curious because it is dedicated to the once famous Jeffcock family. Capt. William Jeffcock was born in 1800 and was a coalmaster in several collieries around Handsworth. He was voted Sheffield's first Lord Mayor in 1843 and went on to build himself "The Towers" in High Hazels Park. He also became a Justice of the Peace and died in 1871. He is buried in a family vault in Handsworth Churchyard not far from the fountain. His brother John Jeffcock was also a Justice of the Peace and was laid to rest in another family grave in Ecclesfield. However, it was John's son, Parkin, born in 1829, who gained national recognition. He was a successful mining engineer who lost his life in 1866 in an attempt to rescue miners trapped by an explosion in the Oaks Pit near Barnsley. The story ran in all the papers and he became something of a hero. Parkin was buried in the family grave in Ecclesfield. Other Jeffcock memorials include a horse trough in Ecclesfield churchyard and a fountain in Ecclesfield Park.

32. A Remnant of Sheffield's Brewing Heritage
CHERRY STREET, S2

Until the mid-eighteenth century, ale (water and grain) and beer (ale and hops) was only brewed commercially on a small scale in the actual premises of public houses. However, between the 1750's and the late nineteenth century, Sheffield witnessed the founding of more than 50 breweries, including such household names as Wards, Stones and Tennants. Comparatively little remains of these enterprises other than the empty premises of Wards on Ecclesall Road and Whitbreads at Lady's Bridge. However, on Cherry Street, off Queen's Road, can be seen part of the original offices of Henry Tomlinson's Anchor Brewery. On one corner there remains the brewery's 'Anchor' motif incorporated into the brickwork. The business was established in 1891, severely damaged in the Blitz of 1940, and in 1942 merged with The Hope Brewery (Claywheels Lane) to form The Hope and Anchor Brewery. In 1954 it was taken over by Truswells and then swallowed up by Bass Charrington in 1963, by which time it included 240 public houses. The Ship Inn, Shalesmoor, still retains Tomlinson's name on its tiled facade. Not far away on Queen's Road is another brewing oddity. The Earl of Arundel and Surrey is Sheffield's only remaining official Pound House where law permits that captured stray animals can be impounded until collection! The two painted shire horses outside remind the passer-by that there are still stables for cart horses at the rear.

33. Fairyland
MACHON BANK, S7

"I am acquainted with at least four places which are known as Machon Bank, "machon" being here equivalent to Maykin, little maid, elle maid, nymph or even witch. The name is evidence of a belief in fays or hillfolk who were once supposed to haunt these places". Thus wrote folklore historian S.O. Addy in his "Household Tales and Other Traditional Remains" published in 1895. It is difficult to imagine Machon Bank, in busy Nether Edge, as being the haunt of such elusive creatures today. However, it is a fascinating pastime to study the often ancient origins of Sheffield's more curious place and street-names. Indeed many hark back to ancient pagan times when man's primitive beliefs were shaped by nature, the seasons and the power of his own imagination. Norton-born Addy goes on to interpret Ecclesall as 'witches hill', and to derive Dobbin Hill/Dobcroft Lane from Dobby, a northern word for goblin. Furthermore, Endcliffe was originally written as El(f)-cliffe, being the haunt of fairies and spirits.

(Flower Fairies™ illustrations copyright © The Estate of Cicely Mary Barker 1940, 1944.)

34. The Futuristic Dairy
BROADFIELD ROAD, S8

Architecturally speaking, Sheffield is best known for its Victorian buildings, as well as those erected since the 1960's. A notable curiosity therefore, is the striking facade of the former Express Dairy on Broadfield Road. Designed and built in 1939 by Hadfield & Cawkwell, its most eyecatching feature is a curved, glazed wall at one end. This is reminiscent of a similar, if larger, wall at the De La Warr Pavilion at Bexhill-on-Sea, built in 1934 by German emigré architect Eric Mendelsohn. Cawkwell is known to have travelled Europe and to have been abreast of the latest fashions in continental architecture. It is likely therefore that European ideas inspired his designs. Indeed, the building still seems ahead of its time today, having aged far more gracefully than its ugly concrete successors thrown up around the city in the sixties. The only criticism of it that the present authors would voice is that the life-size model of a Friesian cow which once stood in the window seems to have been put out to pasture!

35. Home Of The Barrage Balloons
LIGHTWOOD LANE, S8

Few people take much notice of the huge dilapidated sheds on waste ground at Norton, which is used today for driving practice. Fewer still would have imagined that half a century ago these were balloon hangars! The area, still cordoned off in true military style, was once the World War II home of No. 16 Balloon Centre. It formed a crucial part of a ring of hydrogen-filled barrage balloons flown to defend the city and its factories against air attacks. The balloons were tethered by steel cables to winches on the ground and their purpose was to force enemy bombers to fly at higher altitudes. Some aircraft were even damaged by contact with the balloons and cables themselves. The first balloons were flown in August 1939 and the centre was fully functional during the Sheffield Blitz of December 12th 1940. Although many of the 72 balloons were damaged, a full complement was again raised during the second blitz 3 days later. The first crews comprised men of the RAF but later 12-woman crews were formed as more men were needed overseas. It should be noted that there was never a runway at Norton, although an aerodrome was constructed in 1916 at Coal Aston for RFC aircraft. Although long built over, it became for a time No. 2 (Northern) Aircraft Repair Depot.

36. A Pair of Former Mansions
NORTON CHURCH ROAD, S8

The citizens of Sheffield may sometimes express curiosity over how their many wonderful parks came into being. The answer is more often than not a fascinating one tied up with the historical development of the city. This can be demonstrated clearly in the suburb of Norton. In 1925 the magnificent grounds of Norton Hall became Sheffield's largest park when donated by philanthropist J.G. Graves (see no. 16). The Hall had been built in 1815 by banker Samuel Shore, whose family included Florence Nightingale. When his private Church Street bank collapsed in 1850 the estate was bought by Charles Cammell, founder of the famous Cammell, Laird & Co. of shipbuilding fame. Cammell died here in 1879 by which time he had added a colonnade, billiards room and grand dining room. In 1902 the Hall was bought by Bernard Firth, son of steel manufacturer, Mark Firth.

More to do with inherited wealth than any commercial success is the story of Oakes Park off Norton Lane nearby. The Oakes was built originally in c.1670 but remodelled by Sir William Chambers Bagshawe in c.1800. Inhabited by the family for three centuries and once crammed with treasures, it now lies unloved and forlorn though thankfully the estate still provides Sheffield with another of its much loved green spaces. The lake was dug by Napoleonic War prisoners, the terrace designed by Sir Francis Chantrey and the garden designed by John Nash, the architect of Buckingham Palace.

37. A Shropshire Mansion in Sheffield
18 & 20 LINDEN AVENUE, S8

Even to the untrained eye there appears something unusual about this pair of semi-detached houses just off Abbey Lane. Indeed their curious origin has warranted a Grade II listing for them. Called "Preen" and "Wenlock" respectively, part of their fabric was brought from Preen Manor, near Wenlock Edge in Shropshire. The Manor had been built in 1871 by the renowned Victorian architect Norman Shaw. He is best remembered today for his neo-Tudor Cragside Hall, designed for Sir William Armstrong in Northumberland (now a National Trust property). The ornate, half-timbered Preen Manor was demolished in the 1920's and parts were purchased by Sheffield engineer Albert Davidson. Thus, the fine double-gabled facade, as well as a carved crest, came to be incorporated into a pair of Sheffield semis. Who would have guessed!

(N.B. This is a private house and may only be viewed from the roadside).

38. Almshouses for Licensed Victuallers
ABBEYDALE ROAD SOUTH, S17

Opposite the old Dore and Totley railway station is a quaint listed range of buildings immediately recognisable as almshouses (see no. 28). They are curious however in that they were once home to a very specific group of people. The "Sheffield, Rotherham and District Licensed Victuallers Association", that is inn-keepers, had founded a benevolent institution in Grimethorpe in 1844. Using donations from Alderman Thomas Wiley, its function was the maintenance and support of aged and unfortunate association members. A fine memorial to Alderman Wiley was erected outside the institution in 1853. In 1879 a new building was required and so the almshouses at Dore came into being, designed by Sheffield architect John Brightmore Mitchell-Withers. It consisted of 12 houses and a central board room, erected at a cost of £13,000. Each resident received a yearly income plus coal, gas and a vegetable plot. In front of the almshouse can be seen the original memorial to Wiley, brought here from Grimethorpe. In the Great War the building became an Auxiliary Hospital as did the church hall opposite, above whose door is a beautiful clock and mosaic depicting a nurse and a soldier (see back cover bottom).

39. A Derbyshire Custom in South Yorkshire
VICARAGE LANE, S17

Every July, in the Sheffield suburb of Dore, there can be witnessed the ancient Derbyshire custom of Well Dressing (see back cover third down). In the days before piped water, the presence of a spring within a settlement was something to be very thankful for. Accordingly, it is thought that in pagan times, the water spirit would be propitiated by leaving floral garlands around the spring. This was especially important in limestone areas where surface water percolated away very rapidly. Today the tradition is still practised but has evolved into the large floral pictures, usually on a Biblical theme. Created locally, these transient masterpieces comprise petals, leaves, moss and seeds pressed into a board of wet clay. Well dressing at Dore, a village which until recently was part of Derbyshire, is now even more curious as it lies within the modern boundaries of South Yorkshire.

Another Dore oddity is an old boundary stone in the wall of 41 Dore Road, inscribed "A. St. J. C. 1877 no5". The letters stand for "Abbeydale St John's Consolidated Chapelry" (formed 1877) and adorn what was once one of five boundary stones. Another boundary stone, distinguishing Beauchief from Norton, is in the wall of 106 Abbey Lane.

40. The Sheffield Cross
WESTERN BANK, S10

Sheffield's most curious historical artefact can be found in the City Museum at Weston Park. Pride of place amongst the local Bronze Age carved stones and Celtic stone heads is the enigmatic fragmentary Sheffield Cross. It is thought to represent the earliest evidence for religion in Sheffield and was chanced upon in a cutler's town centre workshop early in the nineteenth century. In his fascinating book "Strange South Yorkshire" (1994) author David Clarke suggests it was part of the "Great Cross" which marked the site of a pagan temple where William de Lovetot built the first parish church in c.1100. The Great Cross was destroyed during the Reformation by order of Elizabeth I. Although the original fragment now resides in the British Museum, the plaster cast at Weston Park shows clearly an archer kneeling amidst a vine grove. The attendant decoration of stylised trees and knotwork is typical of ninth century Anglo-Saxon England. Similar work can be seen in abundance in the church porch at Bakewell in Derbyshire. More recent are the carvings over the doorway of Weston Park Museum itself showing the creatures of the world in order of their appearance in time.

41. A Monumental Artist
WESTERN BANK, S10

Sheffield is as famous for its many green spaces as it is for its industrial landscapes. As well as being oases of calm the city's parks contain numerous curiosities, and Weston Park is no exception. There is a statue of Ebenezer Elliott, the Corn Law Rhymer, erected by subscription in 1854 near High Street. It was moved here when the park opened in 1875. Nearby is a stone tablet marking the foundation of part of the University in 1903 by the right honourable Sir Marcus Samuel, Lord Mayor of London. The bandstand is the sole survivor of a once familiar sight in Sheffield's parks, when thousands would attend brass band concerts in the summer months. Most notable however are the monuments to artist Godfrey Sykes (1824-1866). He trained at the Sheffield School of Art before moving to London to work on the decoration of the Victoria and Albert Museum. After his death a column was erected in Weston Park which is a copy of those outside the V&A's lecture theatre, its decorative panels depicting the "Three Ages of Man". Also in his memory are the beautiful lower gateposts on Western Bank, being copies of those used in the V&A's quadrangle where he was working when he died.

42. Memories of a Grand Old Hospital

GLOSSOP ROAD, S10

The most unusual location for a curiosity must surely be the Emergency Admissions Centre of the Royal Hallamshire Hospital on Glossop Road. Supporting the reception desk are four decorated rainwater heads, from the drains of the old Royal Hospital which stood on West Street. That hospital had closed in 1978, having been superseded by the Hallamshire, and been demolished in 1981. All that remains on site is the Mount Zion chapel which had been purchased in 1922 for use as an outpatients department. It was opened by Neville Chamberlain. The hospital itself had been opened in 1895 by the Duke and Duchess of York and been named the Royal Hospital by Queen Victoria. Prior to this grand Renaissance-style building, designed by C. & C.M.E. Hadfield, there had existed the Sheffield Public Hospital, together with a Dispensary which occupied a converted house. Even earlier than this, in 1832, the Dispensary alone had occupied a small home in Tudor Place, where the Central Library now stands. It had opened as a result of the cholera epidemic which had appeared in the same year.

(NB. The Emergency Admissions Centre is a busy and vital part of the hospital and should only be visited with due care and consideration).

43. A Measure of Success
POMONA STREET, S11

An ingenious invention still used to this day in its original form is the spring rewind for pocket measuring tapes. It was the idea of James Chesterman (1792-1867) whose "metallic woven tapes" were made of linen and copper threads. By 1842 he was producing riveted steel tapes but the real breakthrough was yet to come. In 1853, together with Samuel Fox, he developed the heat treatment of continuous steel strip - and the modern steel measuring tape was born. In 1864 the company moved to the Bow Works on Pomona Street, where it remained until 1990, by which time it had become Rabone Chesterman. The works have subsequently become home to the Norwich Union who have been careful to retain the grand street frontage and gateway initialled "J.C.". An informative wall plaque gives details of this historic building.

44. The Beasts of Brincliffe
BRINCLIFFE EDGE ROAD, S11

One of Sheffield's most individual artistic pieces must be the carved tree in Chelsea Park. The dead tree has been covered with beautiful carvings of animals, the main one being an owl with outstretched wings. The sculptor, Jason Thomson, also included a fox, a bat, a dog and ball, and even a tiny beetle. Completed in 1999, the tree is signed by the artist and includes a carved book which reads "The Beasts of Brincliffe" and "Tales of the Edge". The piece was commissioned in 1998 by the Nether Edge Neighbourhood Group in commemoration of its 25th Anniversary. Chelsea Park itself was originally the grounds of Brincliffe Towers, the nearby mansion built in 1852 by James Wilson. Reputedly "the most strongly built house in Sheffield", it later passed into the hands of George Marples and then Robert Styring. In 1925 Styring handed over the estate deeds to the citizens of Sheffield in memory of his wife. After serving as a girls' school and local headquarters for the Royal Army Service Corps, in 1960 the house became a residential home for the elderly. Interestingly, the tree-covered mound in the park was raised to conceal the nearby Nether Edge Workhouse from view!

45. The George Woofindin Almshouses
ECCLESALL ROAD, S11

Nestling idyllically against Brocco Bank and obscured by trees is a curious crescent of picturesque red brick cottages (see back cover top). The eighteen properties, designed by W.R. Bryden and built by John Salt, were erected in 1899-1900, with a further pair being added in 1912. They were financed through the generosity of one George Woofindin, the last surviving son of Richard Woofindin. On his death in 1895, the estate worth c.£120,000 was bequeathed for the erection of the Woofindin Almshouses, as well as a convalescent home in Whiteley Wood. At the time it was the largest sum ever bequeathed to the citizens of Sheffield. Originally built to house the poor, they are now for those people who have lived longest locally, and are administered by Trustees. The listed crescent is approached by a drive and a small bridge across the Porter Brook, which emerges from under Brocco Bank having run the length of nearby Endcliffe Park. The cottages are surprisingly well insulated against the bustle of Ecclesall Road; indeed one of the authors not so long ago glimpsed a heron standing in the river not far from the bus-stop!

46. The Grand Home of a Steel Baron
ENDCLIFFE VALE ROAD, S10

Sure to arouse the curiosity of any passer-by is the fine Italianate style mansion known as Endcliffe Hall. Although it is now military property to which the public have no access, it was originally the grandest of all the homes built for Sheffield's Victorian steel barons. Designed by Flockton & Abbott it was built for Sir John Brown in the 1860's. Brown was born in 1816 in what is now Orchard Square, where a plaque marks the site. Despite a simple education, by the age of 21 he was partner in a cutlery firm. Within a few years he had his own steel business and in 1848 invented the conical steel spring railway buffer. This was soon to be used throughout England's railways and Brown went on to produce half of Britain's railway lines and much of the Navy's armour plate. His huge Atlas works in the East End made him a wealthy man enabling him to employ the city's finest craftsmen at Endcliffe Hall. Most notable were the Grand Staircase murals attributed to Godfrey Sykes. Brown was knighted by Queen Victoria, was Master Cutler twice and Mayor in 1862-63. He eventually sold up and moved to Kent but on his death in 1896 his body was returned to Sheffield to be buried at All Saints in Ecclesall. Endcliffe Hall had cost Brown more than £150,000 to build but was auctioned in 1895 for a mere £26,000. It was later occupied by the Territorial Association for the Hallamshire Battalion (York & Lancaster Regiment). Nearby is Oakbrook, now Notre Dame School, which is a similarly grand house built for Mark Firth. The Prince of Wales, later Edward VII, stayed here when opening Firth Park in 1875.

ENDCLIFFE HALL, SHEFFIELD.

47. An Early Form of Punishment
WHITELEY LANE, S10

In front of the old Fulwood Chapel (1729) on Whiteley Lane can be seen the stocks which once stood on the village green. They are of typical construction comprising two sturdy stone uprights into which are slotted two wooden boards. The ankles of wrongdoers were secured in holes through the board which were then padlocked tightly together. The purpose of the stocks was to shame the culprit by making him look ridiculous in front of passers-by. An Act of Parliament passed in 1350 prescribed the stocks for drunkards, thieves, unruly apprentices and tradesmen who gave short measures. It is not known when the stocks were first used in England although the Anglo-Saxons certainly knew of them. In a charter of 1297 the tenants of Sheffield were granted their own court on the Wicker by Lord Furnival. It is likely that localised punishment, such as a period in the stocks, became commonplace after this time. The last record of the stocks being used in England was at Rugby in 1865. Other stocks in Sheffield can still be seen at Wadsley, Norton and Woodhouse.

48. Memories of H.M.S. Sheffield
CRIMICAR LANE, S10

The city of Sheffield, because of its tremendous steelmaking capacity, has always had close links with the Royal Navy. None has been closer than those with the three ships that have borne proudly the city's name. The first HMS Sheffield was launched in 1936. It was nicknamed *'The Shiny Sheff'* because of its numerous Sheffield stainless steel fittings. The huge cruiser was in the thick of the action during the second world war, being involved in the sinking of the battleships 'Bismarck' and 'Scharnhorst'. After being eventually broken up its tattered battle ensign and bell were placed in the Cathedral. In 1969 'The Shiny Sheff' public house was opened at Lodge Moor and in it can be seen numerous fittings and pieces of fascinating memorabilia from the ship. Not only have ex-crewmembers been re-united here but also survivors of the 'Bismarck'. The second HMS Sheffield was built in 1971. This smaller, but very powerful, destroyer was mortally wounded in 1982 during the Falklands war. However, within a few years a third HMS Sheffield had been built, this time a frigate which remains in service today. The lack of a fitting monument to the brave crews of all three ships was remedied in the year 2000 by the erection of a striking carving in the Cathedral unveiled by HRH The Duke of York *(see frontispiece).*

49. Elliott Rock

LODGE LANE, S10

Were it not for our chancing on an old guidebook, it is likely that this curiosity might well have escaped our attention. The book, entitled "Rambles Round Sheffield" and published by The Sheffield Telegraph nearly a century ago, details a walk through Black Brook Wood, between Hallamshire Golf Course and Manchester Road. Here, in a dark and ancient ravine, were some stepping stones across a brook. Closeby was a large stone jutting out over a waterfall on which were carved the enigmatic words "ELLIOTT ROCK". After much exploration we can confirm that the rock, albeit weathered, still exists, recently cleared of moss by the local Victorian Society. The name is that of poet Ebenezer Elliott, born near Rotherham in 1781. He rose from destitution to become a successful iron merchant with a fine house in Upperthorpe. He was also a celebrated poet remembered chiefly for his poems condemning the Corn Laws. Elliott also extolled the rural delights of Hallamshire, especially Rivelin, and would often sit on the rock in Black Brook Wood for inspiration. A century ago the rock was a popular tourist attraction, as old postcards of the period show. Today, we were lucky to find it at all.

> "Beautiful river! goldenly shining,
> Where with the cistus woodbines are twining;
> (Birklands around thee, mountains above thee)
> Rivelin wildest! do I not love thee?"

50. A Great Sculptor's Early Works
INFIRMARY ROAD, S6

Despite its size, Sheffield has surprisingly little monumental sculpture in its centre and immediate surroundings. All the more precious therefore are two survivals at the former Infirmary. Designed by John Rowsthorne the General Infirmary was built in the 1790's by public subscription in what was then Upperthorpe Meadows. The impressive facade has bow windows, a pediment and a porticoed main entrance. Either side of the portico are two carved niches containing the sculptured figures of "Hope" and "Charity". These are early works by Francis Chantrey of Norton, one of England's greatest sculptors. The Royal Infirmary closed its doors in 1980 having been superseded by the Royal Hallamshire Hospital but the statues remain. Other buildings of note which made up the original infirmary complex are the Round House, formerly an outpatients' ward, and Centenary House, which was once a nurses' home. Also unusual are the stables and coach house of Joseph Tomlinson, a Victorian horse bus operator and funeral director. His former premises can be seen across Infirmary Road at Borough Mews at the end of Bedford Street.

51. The Mousehole Forge
RIVELIN VALLEY ROAD, S6

The Rivelin Valley Nature Trail is fascinating in itself, but also of considerable interest to the industrial archaeologist. Amongst the trees where Stannington Road and Rivelin Valley Road converge, can be found the remains of the Mousehole Forge, now lovingly restored by the present owners to a private house. The site began as a lead-smelting mill early in the seventeenth century but soon became an iron forge. The Bamforth family, who owned the site for two centuries, leased the forge to the Cockshutts of Huthwaite (1740's-90's). It was at this time that the world-renowned Mousehole anvils were made. Bearing their unmistakeable "mousehole" trademark, the anvils were in great demand abroad, especially in America. To this day, anvil enthusiasts wax lyrical about Mousehole anvils! From 1827 the forge was owned by M&H Armitage, during which time it suffered damage from the Sheffield Flood. Other owners came and went until eventual bankruptcy and closure in 1933. However, the house, hand-forge, wheelpits and watercourses remain, as does the enthusiasm for the anvils produced here 200 years ago.

(NB. This building is privately owned but can be viewed from the iron gates. For a closer look please seek permission first.)

52. Waterwheels and Weirs
STANNINGTON ROAD, S6

By looking over the wall at the bottom of Stannington Road, across from Holme Lane in Malin Bridge, a water wheel can be seen amongst the trees which has had a long and fascinating history. Often referred to as the "Old Corn Mill Water Wheel", it is notably curious in being a rare example of an 'undershot' wheel. That is, the water from the nearby weir, used to turn the wheel, passed below it, and not over the top as was more common. Between 1739 and 1864 it was used to power grinding wheels for sharpening knives. It was in 1864 however, that the mill was severely damaged by water from the Great Sheffield Flood. After being rebuilt it continued as a grinding shop until German Wilson converted it into a machine shop and sawmill. Later still in 1905 his son turned it into a corn mill. Like Sheffield's many other watermills, it was eventually outmoded and fell into disrepair, its wheel tumbling into the river. However, it escaped demolition and this important industrial artefact was restored by Mr. D. Marsden. Today, although no longer connected to any machinery, the wheel can still be seen together with old millstones outside the building *(pictured)*. Other former wheels along the once busy Loxley Valley, albeit of the 'overshot' type, exist at Low Matlock Lane and further upstream at Olive Wheel. The former is the only water-powered steel rolling mill left in Western Europe.

53. Evidence of the Sheffield Flood
PENISTONE ROAD, S6

So much has been written elsewhere about the Great Sheffield Flood that only a few facts are needed here. The collapse of the Dale Dyke Reservoir, near Bradfield, occurred on the night of 11th-12th March, 1864. The resulting wall of water hurtled down into Hillsborough via the Loxley Valley and on into the city centre. In all 240 people died, c.700 animals were lost, 100 or more buildings levelled and 4000 homes damaged. Surprisingly, any memorials of this catastrophic event are few and far between. Most graphic are wall plaques marking the depth of water. These can be seen at The Shakespeare and The Old Blue Balls pubs, as well as Morrison's supermarket in the Barracks *(pictured)*. Now lost are plaques in the old Vickers works at Millsands and an old building on Green Lane. Near the site of the dam itself are stones marked "C.L.O.B." ("Centre Line of Old Bank") together with a memorial plaque erected by The Bradfield Historical Society. Most poignant however are the numerous gravestones to victims of the "inundation". These can be found in Wadsley Parish churchyard, the churchyard of the former Loxley United Reformed Church, and the churchyard of St John the Baptist, Chapeltown. A relic from a recent and far lesser flood is a large log washed onto platform 5 of the Midland Railway Station on December 21st, 1991. It is still there to-day!

54. An Ancient Cruck Barn
OAKS LANE, S5

Following the Norman invasion in 1066 the so-called 'cruck' system of building became widespread. A cruck is a sturdy pair of curving timbers set at ground level and meeting at the top. Several pairs would be set out and connected at the apex by a ridge purlin. Further purlins were attached down to gutter level, at right angles to which were attached the rafters. A thatched roof could then be added. Below gutter level, the space between the crucks would be filled with wattle and daub. Later the walls may have been rebuilt in stone and the thatch replaced by stone tiles. Sheffield is fortunate in that several good examples of cruck-built structures have survived. The best is just inside the western entrance to Concord Park and is thought to date from the twelfth century. Other examples include Cannon Hall, Totley; the Herdings, Norton; outbuildings at Whirlow Hall Farm; a barn on Wilson Place, off Gleadless Road; and a barn on Oldfield Road, Stannington. It should be said, however, that often the crucks are only visible from inside the building.

55. The Sword Dancers
MAIN STREET, GRENOSIDE, S30

In both Handsworth and Grenoside the curious and ancient custom of 'sword dancing' can still be witnessed. It occurs on Boxing Day and its murky origins may extend back as far as the Vikings or Celts. This mid-winter ritual celebrates the Winter Solstice, the end of the old year and coming of the new, the death and return of the sun. Although the present dance is a revival dating to Victorian times, it may originally have been part of a more elaborate "mumming" ceremony including a play. At Grenoside, the sword dance is held outside the Old Harrow Inn on Main Street at 11am on Boxing Day *(pictured)*. To the sound of a fiddler the captain and his six men dance in a ring, their iron-shod clogs beating a rhythm on the ground. Each dancer, resplendent in his colourful tunic, grasps his neighbour's sword, all six eventually linked aloft by the Captain in a spectacular "lock". The Captain then falls to the ground, his fox-fur hat "decapitated" beside him, representing the symbolic death of one year. However, he soon recovers from this ritual sacrifice, hope returns and the dancers repair to the inn for suitable refreshment. The new year is already starting in style!
(NOTE: The Handsworth uniforms and dance routines differ somewhat from those described above.)

56. Of Boggards and Barghasts!
BOGGARD LANE, S30

In olden times, when the world was a more mysterious and often fearsome place, phantoms were a very real threat. They appeared in all shapes and sizes with a variety of regional names. The 'barghast', for example, was a ferocious black dog with eyes the size of saucers! Equally dangerous was the north-country 'boggard', which could take the form of a wandering dog or headless figure. Typically they lurked at secluded crossroads, on country lanes and even entered remote cottages at night, putting a clammy hand on a sleeping person's face. At Worrall, near Oughtibridge, such an occurrence is said to have inspired an old trackway to be called Boggard Lane. Another boggard frequented Bunting Nook, near Norton Church, where legend claims no birds will sing. Both locations, if visited on a suitably windswept autumn evening, can still leave the calmest traveller looking over their shoulder!

Further Reading:

A Popular History of Sheffield (J. Edward Vickers), E P Publishing, 1978
A Guide to the Industrial History of South Yorkshire (Derek Bayliss), Assoc. For Industrial Archaeology, 1995
A Pub On Every Corner (Douglas Lamb), The Hallamshire Press, 1997
Central Sheffield in Old Photographs (Martin Olive), Alan Sutton, 1994
Images of Sheffield (Sheffield Newspapers), Breedon Books, 1993
Lest We Forget (Douglas Lamb), Pickards Publishing, 1998
Listed Buildings of Sheffield (Barbara A. West), The Hallamshire Press, 1998
More Images of Sheffield (Sheffield Newspapers), Breedon Books, 1994
Norton in Wartime, Norton History Group, 1995
Sheffield Curiosities (Duncan and Trevor Smith), The Ridings Press, 1999
South and West Yorkshire Curiosities (Duncan and Trevor Smith), The Dovecote Press, 1992
Strange Sheffield (David Clarke and Rob Wilson), ASSAP, 1987
Strange South Yorkshire (David Clarke), Sigma Press, 1994
The History of The City of Sheffield 1843-1993 (Clyde Binfield et al), Sheffield Academic Press, 1993

The offices of the Sheffield United Gaslight Company, Commercial Street (see No. 16)

Acknowledgements:

Angela Shawcroft (for typing the manuscript), Tim and Jane Hale & family, The Sheffield Postcard Company, Julie MacNamara, Peter Carter, Brian and Maureen Eyles, Roswitha Reisinger, Mary Smith, Terry Green, Fiona Crownshaw, Jan & Dave Thomasson and Barbara White ("The Shiny Sheff" public house), Janet Goddard (Emergency Admissions Centre, Royal Hallamshire Hospital), Victor Povid, Gillian Pritchard (Sheffield Cathedral Guide), John and Julia Hatfield (Mousehole Forge), the volunteers of The South Yorkshire Fire Service Museum, Frederick Warne & Co., and the very helpful staff of the Local Studies Department of Sheffield City Library.